DATE DUE

Colonial Virginia

Mitchell Lane
PUBLISHERS

P.O. Box 196 • Hockessin, Delaware 19707

Titles in the Series

Colonial Virginia

Susan Sales Harkins and
William H. Harkins

Printing   1   2   3   4   5   6   7   8   9

Library of Congress Cataloging-in-Publication Data
Harkins, Susan Sales.
    Colonial Virginia / by Susan Sales Harkins and William H. Harkins.
        p. cm. — (Building America)
    Includes bibliographical references and index.
    ISBN 978-1-58415-548-5 (library bound)
    1. Virginia—History—Colonial period, ca. 1600–1775—Juvenile literature.
I. Harkins, William H. II. Title.
F229.H2735 2007
975.5'02—dc22

                                                                    2007000665

ABOUT THE AUTHORS: Susan and William Harkins live in Kentucky, where they enjoy writing together for children. Susan has written many books for adults and children. William is a history buff. In addition to writing, he is a member of the Air National Guard.

PHOTO CREDITS: Cover, pp. 1, 3—North Wind Picture Archives; pp. 6, 9 (left)—Barbara Marvis; pp. 9 (right), 17—NASA; p. 10—Paulus van Somer; pp. 12, 18—JupiterImages; p. 15—Hans Musil/Creative Commons; p. 20 map—Jonathan Scott; p. 23—Getty Images; p. 26—APVA-Preservation Virginia; pp. 28, 33, 34, 36—North Wind Picture Archives; p. 41—Peter Rothermel/Patrick Henry National Memorial.

PUBLISHER'S NOTE: This story is based on the authors' extensive research, which they believe to be accurate. Documentation of such research is contained on page 46.

The internet sites referenced herein were active as of the publication date. Due to the fleeting nature of some web sites, we cannot guarantee they will all be active when you are reading this book.

                                                                    PLB

Contents

*For Your Information

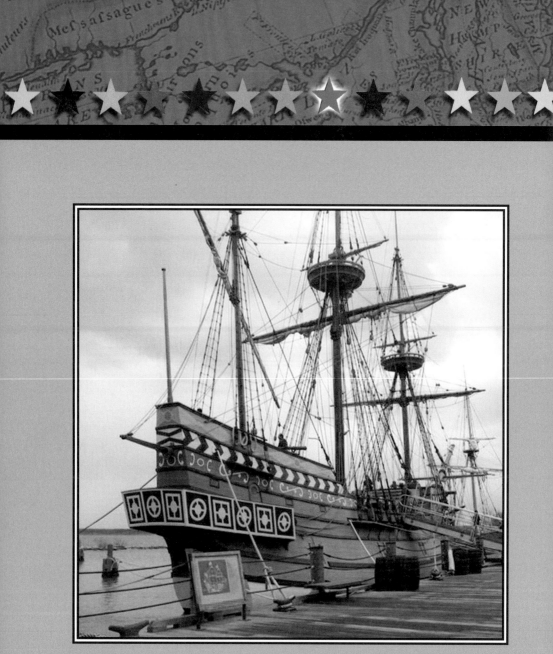

A replica of the Susan Constant is accurate in size and detail. Replicas of all three of the small sailing vessels that made their way from England to North America travel the eastern seacoast, joining festivals and other community events.

Chapter

1

Finding Virginia

Just before dawn, three small ships approached the Chesapeake Bay. By the light of a nearly full moon, the flagship's leadsman took soundings. As the ships sailed into shallow water, he took no breaks from his task. It was his job to measure the depth of the water. If the water became too shallow, they would run aground.

Fortunately, the weather was mild. Gentle waves slapped at the bottom of the ships. Sails popped in a calm spring breeze. Only the leadsman calling out each new measurement broke the silence.

Storms the week before had blown them off course. Even Captain Christopher Newport wasn't sure where they were. Captain John Ratcliffe wanted to give up the search and return home to England.[1] They all hoped that the shallow readings meant they were close to land.

Anxious passengers stood silently on deck, leaning into the darkness and hoping for their first glimpse of land. They could smell it, heavy with spring. They just couldn't see anything through the darkness.

Those standing closest to the leadsman could hear the rope whining in the wind as he twirled the lead line in a huge vertical circle.

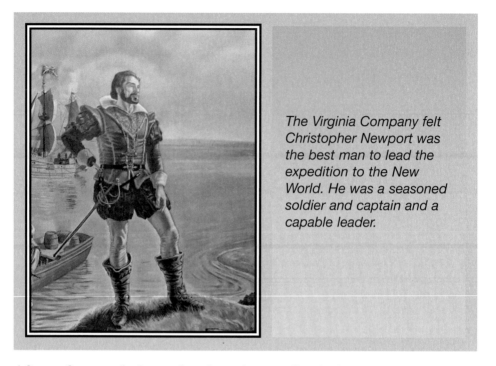

The Virginia Company felt Christopher Newport was the best man to lead the expedition to the New World. He was a seasoned soldier and captain and a capable leader.

After a few revolutions, they heard a small splash as he cast the lead weight into the water just ahead of the ship.

Then they all waited. It was dangerous enough approaching land you could see. Approaching it at night was treacherous.

Finally, dawn's faint beams broke the tension. There, straight ahead, was the coast of North America. "Land ho!" came the jubilant cry. The men were overjoyed but exhausted. They had reached Virginia!

By daybreak, the *Susan Constant*, the *Discovery*, and the *Godspeed* slipped quietly into the Chesapeake Bay. England was about to make its presence known in the New World.

All three ships dropped anchor just inside the mouth of the bay. After a four-month voyage in cramped quarters and deplorable conditions, the men were too tired to celebrate.

Captain Newport took a small group of about thirty men exploring.[2] They named the small point of land they explored Cape Henry in honor of King James' eldest son.[3] They fashioned a cross from driftwood and planted it in the ground, claiming Cape Henry for the Church of England and King James I.

Replicas of Discovery *(left) and* Godspeed *(right) were similar in size to the Norman flatboats used to invade England more than five centuries earlier (in 1066).*

Just past the beach and the sand dunes, the men entered a dense spring forest. It seemed like paradise. The woods rang with the songs of wild birds. The air was fragrant with spring blossoms. Old vines hung thick with ripening berries. Wild game and deer were abundant. Rushing streams of cool water refreshed the men as they explored.

Men on board the three anchored ships took turns watching for the explorers to return. At sundown, they saw movement behind the dunes. They watched as Captain Newport and his men, standing at the top of the dunes, paused for a moment. Looking behind, they all watched the forest fade into darkness.

As they crossed the beach, the small party of explorers could still make out the shapes of the three ships anchored in the bay. They didn't see another small group of men creeping on all fours behind the dunes. Each of these men clutched a bow in his mouth.

England was slow to explore and settle the New World. The French and the Spanish both tried settlements in the mid-sixteenth century. It wasn't until James I became king that England successfully settled the area Elizabeth I named Virginia.

Suddenly, terrifying whoops and cries filled the night. Arrows flew, striking the English explorers. They were under attack!

Quickly, the men on board ship fired a cannon. Its powerful boom shook the small cove. The natives quickly disappeared into the woods, which echoed with their war cries as they retreated.[4]

The Englishmen wasted no time returning to the ship, not knowing whether the hostile natives meant to return. Two adventurers lay bleeding and crying out in pain, the arrows still piercing their flesh.

England had definitely found a paradise—a land with plenty of natural resources. Virginia also held death for most of England's first settlers. The small war party of the native Paspahegh was just the beginning of their troubles. Things would get much worse for the settlers. It was April 26, 1607. By the end of the year, two thirds of these adventurous men would be dead.

The Voyage to the New World

Virginia's first settlers sailed across the Atlantic Ocean in three small and primitive sailing vessels. The Virginia Company of London chose Captain Christopher Newport to lead the expedition from the flagship, the *Susan Constant*. He had spent years fighting the Spanish as a privateer—even losing an arm to his enemy.

Captains John Ratcliffe and Bartholomew Gosnold had charge of the *Discovery* and the *Godspeed*, respectively. Captain Newport was the only captain of the three to return to England. In fact, Captain Ratcliffe died a horrible death at the hands of the Powhatan Indians just a few years after arriving in Virginia.

Storms trapped the ships off the coast of England, where they waited for six weeks for fair weather.[5] By then, many of the men were ready to return home. Captain Newport, with the help of John Smith and Reverend Robert Hunt, convinced the passengers to continue.[6] Another storm in the West Indies blew them slightly off course, further delaying their arrival in Virginia.

The four-month journey was utterly miserable. The ships were so small that most of the men ate and slept on deck. The hulls of all three ships were full of food and supplies. The largest ship, the *Susan Constant,* wasn't much bigger than a modern home. Yet approximately seventy passengers and crewmen made that four-month journey on the Susan Constant.

Without refrigeration, the men ate dried meats and stale, weevil-infested biscuits. After the first few days, there was no fresh water. They drank ale for most of the trip. There was no modern sanitation, although the men did use a primitive toilet. Many of the men were often seasick. After just a few days, the smell was unbearable. There was no place where the men could escape the smell of sweaty bodies, human waste, and vomit.

The landing of the three ships at Jamestown and the building of Fort James

Elizabeth I took the throne of England during troubled times. She was hopeful that England would settle North America, but she couldn't finance a serious settlement venture. The best she could do was to coax a few men to explore the country, at their own expense.

Chapter

For Honor, Glory, and Profit!

Virginia's first English settlers were ill prepared for their journey into history. Prior to the Virginia Company of London, England had sent few explorers to the Western Hemisphere. They knew almost nothing of the country's climate and native peoples. After Christopher Columbus bumped into the American continent in 1492, England waited over one hundred years to stake its claim in America.

When Elizabeth I inherited her crown in 1558, England was bankrupt. Mary of Guise of Scotland threatened Elizabeth's future by claiming Elizabeth's crown for her daughter, Mary. Elizabeth had no money to fund an army. War and religious persecution had left her people bruised and battered.

Her subjects had no more money than her royal treasury. Peasants starved, but that wasn't the real problem—peasants always starved. England had stopped moving forward. Instead of leading the world in commerce, the English killed one another over God. She had her father, Henry VIII, and her sister, Mary I, to thank for England's perilous and fragile state.

Although Elizabeth inherited a troubled country, she proved herself a fair and able ruler. She improved trade, and England began to

Mary of Guise was ambitious and believed her daughter Mary to be the true heir to the English throne. The matter was settled decades later when the daughter, who was also Elizabeth's cousin, visited the Queen of England. Elizabeth jailed her in the Tower of London and later had her beheaded.

prosper again. She put an end to religious persecution and war. Most importantly, she encouraged her subjects to educate themselves. An informed people would be less likely to kill one another over religious differences. At least she hoped that would be the case.

Despite her efforts, England's poor continued to struggle. The aristocracy's practice of enclosure—fencing in previously common land—was destroying England's small farms. For hundreds of years, common rights to open lands allowed small farmers to graze their livestock; to hunt for pigs, wild game, and berries; and to gather wood for fuel. Farmers and peasants depended on these rights for their livelihoods and their meals. Wild game filled their stomachs and open pastures fed their cattle. As profits for English wool grew, common lands shrank. The aristocratic landlords built fences to keep their sheep in and to keep the peasants out.

The Church of England and the government were against enclosure, but the aristocracy didn't care. Their lands were common only by practice. Legally, no one could stop the landlords from fencing in their property. Farmers and peasants, once able to live off the land, moved to the cities, where they tried to find work as unskilled laborers.

The social change alarmed everyone with any sense. Less than 5 percent of England's people belonged to the rich ruling class known as the aristocracy. These nobles lived in elaborate palaces, rode about the city in carriages, and wore silk clothing. Servants took care of their every need.

The remaining 95 percent of the population were mostly poor. Merchants had some money and property. They were commoners, and there weren't a lot of them. Small farmers and shopkeepers owned a little property but seldom had money. At the bottom of England's social heap were the peasants. They were unskilled and owned no property.

About 80 percent of England's people lived in villages or on farms. Approximately one-half of the rural peasants lost their land between 1530 and 1630.[1] They ended up in the cities, where they begged when they couldn't find work. Often, they resorted to crime. London grew from 120,000 people in 1550 to 200,000 in 1600.[2]

The famous Canterbury Cathedral was built by Pope Gregory during the sixth century. A thousand years later, the church still influenced everyday life, but had less political clout.

Thanks to Elizabeth, England's economy was growing, but not fast enough to support the displaced farmers and peasants from the countryside. Competition for jobs in the cities forced wages down and rents up. More and more peasants depended on charity. As the numbers of poor increased, so did the special charity tax. Those with money and property began to fear a social and economic disaster if something didn't change.

England had to expand or collapse. At least, that was the warning from the West Country Men (so called because most of them lived in the western counties of England, and because they hoped to settle Virginia, which lay to the west across the Atlantic Ocean). This small band of rich adventurers promoted the New World as the answer to England's problems.

They suggested that England send its poor to Virginia. There, they could produce goods to sell in England and Europe. The poor would have jobs and a chance at a better life. Investors would make money off the goods Virginia exported. It was a sound plan. There is nothing to suggest that these men were anything but sincere in their plans.

Elizabeth also heard tales of the New World's great wealth. She knew that the Spanish filled their treasury with plundered gold. England should have a share of that wealth too, but she couldn't finance such a venture. Instead, she called on the West Country Men to explore and settle the land between modern-day Maine and Florida—at their own expense, of course. Men like Sir Francis Drake, Sir Walter Ralegh, and Sir Humphrey Gilbert were willing to spend their own money for the opportunities waiting in Virginia. (*Ralegh* is often spelled *Raleigh*. However, he spelled his name *Ralegh*.) Elizabeth named the wilderness Virginia after herself, England's virgin queen.

Another opportunity to increase profits in England lay in finding the Northwest Passage. If found, the passage would make trade with Asia quicker and easier. The plan was to sail northwest from England to the Indies, instead of south and then east around the tip of Africa. In 1576, Elizabeth sent Martin Frobisher to search for the Northwest Passage. It wasn't an attempt to colonize Virginia, but he did explore northeastern Canada.

For five centuries, Europeans tried to find a western route to Asia. Known as the Northwest Passage, many sixteenth-century explorers tried to find it through North America, but failed. Roald Amundsen of Norway finally discovered the elusive passage in 1906, through the icy waters of the Arctic Circle.

When Frobisher failed to the find the passage, Elizabeth granted Sir Humphrey Gilbert a patent in June 1578 to found a colony at Newfoundland. After Gilbert ran out of money, Sir Walter Ralegh tried.

In 1585, Ralegh sent a small group of men to Virginia. They ended up on Roanoke, a small island along the coast of today's North Carolina. Conditions were so harsh that they quickly abandoned their settlement and returned to England. Ralegh tried again in 1587. This time, he sent 100 colonists. In 1590, John White, the colony's leader, returned to Roanoke with supplies from England. He found the small village abandoned. He never found the settlers. We still don't know what happened to Roanoke's colonists, and we probably never will.

Elizabeth died in 1603, without seeing a permanent English settlement in Virginia. In 1606, the new king of England, James I, granted a charter for the southern half of North America to the Virginia Company of London, later called the Virginia Company. Investors provided the money necessary to fund a permanent English settlement in Virginia. In return, investors would share the colony's profits. America's first English colony was a business venture, not a royal undertaking.

Late that same year, a small group of brave and adventurous Englishmen tried again. This time, they planned to settle in the

Sir Walter Ralegh was one of the first to support England's involvement in the New World. Twice he financed colonies at Roanoke, but both failed. For his devotion to Elizabeth I, he eventually lost his head. She forbade him to go to Virginia. He ignored it, and as punishment, she had him executed.

Chesapeake Bay area. They believed that the bay and its tributaries would support sound harbors and supply abundant food.

Approximately 100 English gentlemen, craftsmen, laborers, and servants left England in December of 1606 to establish Jamestown in Virginia. Leaving their lives in England behind, they crossed the Atlantic in three small ships: the *Susan Constant*, the *Godspeed*, and the *Discovery*. Few of them saw England again.

Virginia provided several firsts for England. The colony was the first permanent English settlement in the New World. For the first time, the government, in the form of the Virginia Company of London, moved its citizens to a new land. Perhaps most importantly, the first representative government in the Western Hemisphere emerged in Virginia, giving birth to American common law.[3]

The Virginia Company of London

Quebec
(France, 1608)

Port Royal
(France, 1605)

Popham Colony
(England, 1607)

41°

Atlantic
Ocean

38°

Jamestown
(England, 1607)

**Early Settlements
in North America**

St. Augustine
(Spain, 1565)

Plymouth Company ▬
London Company ▬
Granted to both ▭

James I awarded a charter to a group of investors known as the Virginia Company of London. They sold shares in the company to fund a voyage to the New World. Their goal was to make a profit for the company. From a Virginia settlement, the English could search for a water passage to the Pacific Ocean. They also planned to plunder the Spanish West Indies from Virginia's coast. Settling the land was a part of their plan, but whatever made the most profit would get the company's support.

Settlers agreed to work for the company in return for their passage to Virginia. The company supplied arms, clothing, and food. It was risky for the settlers, but the poor had no hope of improving their lives in England.

With no previous experience in colonization, the company made mistakes. A council of seven men controlled the settlers. The council assigned jobs, divided the food, and even punished settlers as needed. Most were incompetent. With poor leadership, Virginia wasn't an overnight success. The settlers spent most of their energy just trying to survive the wilderness and hide from hostile natives.

In 1614, the seven-year term of service for the first settlers expired. Those who stayed received small tracts of land on tenure. By the end of 1614, there were 81 tenant farms in Virginia. This was a boon for the colonists, who began growing tobacco for their own profit. It wasn't so good for the company, because tenant farmers no longer worked for the company.

Even with the tenant farmers, there weren't enough people to work the colony. In 1616, there were only 351 men, women, and children in the whole colony.[4] The company still sent food and other supplies to help the settlers survive. By 1618, the company was heavily in debt, owing almost 9,000 British pounds.[5]

Between 1619 and 1623, around 4,000 settlers emigrated to Virginia. By the spring of 1623, there were only 1,275 left.[6] During those four years, the colony's death rate was 75 percent. Under charges of mismanagement and negligence, James I revoked the company's charter on May 24, 1624. That action made Virginia a royal colony.

19

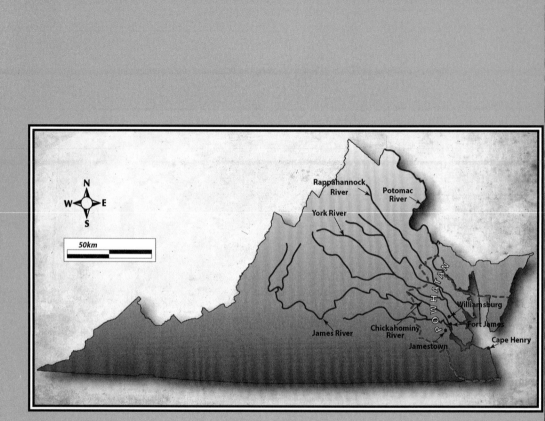

After both colonies at Roanoke failed, the Virginia Company sent men to settle the Chesapeake Bay area. They settled a small peninsula on the north side of the James River.

Chapter

3

Virginia, "Earth's Onely Paradise"

The first English settlers expected to find friendly natives with whom they could trade for food and labor. Their first encounter was anything but friendly. Hostile Paspahegh Indians attacked the first settlers to set foot in Virginia.

On board the *Susan Constant*, the settlers were eager to hear about Virginia. Most of the men in that first exploration party were disappointed. They found none of the gold and silver the company had promised. Instead, they spent the day foraging through dense forests, as reported by George Percy: "wee could find nothing worth the speaking of, but faire meddowes and goodly tall Trees, with such Fresh-waters running through the woods, as I was almost ravished at the first sight thereof."[1] He called it "Earth's Onely Paradise."[2]

Tensions were high by the time Captain Newport finally opened the sealed box, which held instructions for the settlers. Before leaving England, officials of the Virginia Company had given Newport the box, with strict orders not to open it until they reached Virginia.

A letter inside named the settlement's first governing council: Edward-Maria Wingfield, Christopher Newport, Bartholomew Gosnold, John Ratcliffe, George Kendall, John Martin, and John Smith.

The first six members of the council quickly rejected Smith's appointment. Smith was a prisoner, accused of plotting mutiny during the voyage. They elected Wingfield president of the new council. As an educated man, he seemed a good choice. Unfortunately for the settlement, he was incompetent and arrogant.

The colony's main goal was to make money for the Virginia Company. The company's instructions were clear:

- Choose a site that is accessible by water but far enough inland to be safe from the Spanish.
- Plant a garden to supply food.
- Search for the Northwest Passage.
- Search for gold.

In addition, they had strict orders not to offend the native people: "In all your passages you must have great care not to offend the naturals."[3] The English didn't want to conquer the natives as the Spanish had. England wanted to "civilize" them, convert them to Christianity, and exploit them as laborers.

Eventually, the council settled on a small peninsula on the north shore of the James River. Much of the time the peninsula was an island as high tide covered the narrow bridge of land that connected it to the mainland. They called their settlement Fort James. On May 13, 1607, they began moving provisions to their new home.

Captain Newport's men explored the James River, which they named for King James I. The southeastern Chesapeake Bay has three other major tributaries besides the James: the York, the Rappahannock, and the Potomac Rivers. The settlers had no way of knowing it at the time, but nearly 24,000 natives lived along these rivers. They called themselves Powhatans (POW-uh-tans). Although John Smith was still under arrest for mutiny, he joined Newport's party. They needed every able man to work.

While Captain Newport's party explored, the council's president, Wingfield, put the men to work looking for gold. At night they slept in bark shacks and tents. It was the first of many mistakes President Wingfield would make.

To make matters worse, not all the men worked. About half of the settlers were gentlemen, and their contribution to the settlement was to eat the group's food. The Virginia Company had intended to re-create English society in Virginia, which was an arrogant mistake. The colony needed laborers, farmers, and fishermen, not idle gentlemen with large appetites and egos.

In late May, Newport's party returned to find several men wounded and at least one man dead. Hostile warriors who laid claim to the small island had attacked the fort. Smith was furious and publicly blamed the council. Most of the settlers were quick to champion Smith for challenging the council. They demanded that the council allow Smith to take his appointed seat as one of its members.

Everyone blamed President Wingfield for the attack. He forbade the men to build a protective wall around the settlement. He also refused to move stores of weapons still aboard ship into the settlement. Wingfield argued that a wall and weapons would have frightened the local inhabitants. When the settlers realized just how vulnerable they were, they began working to surround the fort with a triangular wall of thick, upright logs. They shaved the tip of each log into a sharp point. They positioned a cannon in each corner to fortify the wall.

James Fort was built close to the banks of the James River. The water was deep, and small ships could moor right next to the bank.

When they finished, Wingfield put them to work cutting clapboard, which they sent back to England. There was no time to build themselves proper huts or shelters or to start a plot of vegetables.

Their stores of food were running low. Each man's daily ration was grain and bread. With the surrounding woods full of wild game, nuts, and berries, they were starving. The local Paspahegh Indians were hostile and harassed the men if they left the fort. Besides, most of the men came from England's cities. Some of them had skills, but they weren't hunters and fishermen.

By summer, their Eden on the James River was a mosquito-filled swamp. Summer tides turned the river's freshwater brackish. They had been too busy digging for gold and cutting clapboard to dig a well. They had no choice but to drink from the salty river. Many grew sick from salt poisoning. Others fell ill with mosquito-borne diseases, such as dysentery and malaria. Everyone languished in the sweltering heat. All work stopped. The healthier men were too busy tending the sick to work. In August alone, nineteen men died of disease or from wounds inflicted by hostile natives.[4] The council arrested President Wingfield and elected John Ratcliffe their new president.

A chance meeting probably saved the settlement. The settlers became anxious when Captain Newport didn't return from England in November, as scheduled. Smith took a few men and sailed up the Chickahominy River, hoping to trade for food. Several miles upriver, a group of Powhatan warriors killed Smith's companions and took him prisoner.

On December 30, Smith met the great chief, Powhatan. (Powhatan was his title, not his given name.) Smith stood in front of the old man in his warm and smoky lodge for a long time. Powhatan contemplated his choices. Perhaps he could trade food for the white settlers' guns and cannons. On the other hand, these men were weak and he felt no respect for them. If he killed them or let them starve, Powhatan could take their weapons.

Smith claimed later that at Powhatan's signal, two large warriors pushed him to the ground. Other men brandishing wooden clubs lunged toward him, but before their clubs smashed his skull, a young girl threw herself across his body. Matoaka, Powhatan's favorite daughter, saved Smith from death. Powhatan called this favored child Pocahontas or "naughty one."

Eventually Smith returned to the settlement with food from the Powhatans. The council promptly arrested him for murder. They didn't believe his story of Powhatan and Pocahontas. They planned to hang him the next day. Fortunately for Smith, Captain Newport returned from England the same day and freed Smith.

Captain Newport found only 38 of the original 104 men still alive at Fort James. Two thirds of the original settlers died from starvation, disease, or wounds inflicted by hostile natives.

Over the next few years, Pocahontas was a frequent visitor to the fort. She taught Smith her language, and he taught her English. Often, she brought food for the settlers, who traded beads and kettles for corn.

The settlers and Powhatan kept a tense peace, but the fort languished. In July 1608, Smith took control of the colony. Under his leadership, the men built decent shelters and dug a well. Many still died of disease. Smith traded with the native peoples for food, but it was never enough. He insisted that settlers work if they wanted to eat.

Tragedy struck Smith in the summer of 1609, when his powder bag caught fire. The burn was so severe that he returned to England for treatment. That winter was also tragic for the settlers Smith left behind. Powhatan, who had respected Smith, murdered Ratcliffe, the colony's new president, when he tried to trade for food. Without Smith to negotiate with the local people, the settlers starved. They ate their horses, their pets, and even rats. Settlers came to call this winter the Starving Time, as later reported by John Smith in his memoirs: "This was that time which still to this day we called 'the starving time.' It was too vile to say, and scarce to be believed what we endured. But the occasion was our own, for want of providence, industry, and government and not the barrenness and defect of the country, as is generally supposed."[5] (Smith repeated the story as told to him in later years by other settlers.) A few even resorted to a form of cannibalism. One settler reported: "so great was our famine that a savage we slew and buried, the poorer sort took him up again and ate him."[6]

After his arrival in Jamestown in 1619, Governor George Yeardley announced that the Virginia Colony would establish the first legislative assembly in the New World. The House of Burgesses met for the first time on July 30, 1619.

The following spring (1610), the emaciated settlers abandoned the fort and tried to return to England. The colony's first governor, Lord De La Warr, arrived just in time with new supplies.

An unexpected event brought a tentative peace in 1614, when Pocahontas married John Rolfe, an English planter. The English settlers were still struggling to find some way to make the colony profitable. It was Rolfe who finally made that happen. By crossbreeding tobacco, he produced a superior blend. Within a few years, Virginia's farmers were growing tobacco almost exclusively.[7]

By 1616, Virginia had four hundred settlers living in four settlements: James City (Jamestown), Henrico, Charles City, and Kecoughtan (Elizabeth City).[8] The colony was still too small, so the Virginia Company started the headright system. In 1618, any settler paying his own passage to Virginia received fifty acres of land. The number of settlers increased quickly.

All those people needed a more realistic form of government, so the Virginia Company replaced the colony's martial law with North America's first legislative assembly. On July 30, 1619, Governor George Yeardley convened the House of Burgesses in Jamestown for the first time.[9]

The Powhatan People

In 1607, English settlers found a well-established culture of native peoples living in the Chesapeake Bay area. At the time, there were about thirty Algonquian tribes led and ruled by Wahunsonacock (Wah-hun-sen-uh-kaw), the Chief Powhatan. They farmed, fished, hunted, and gathered wild foods. They weren't nomadic, but they did move with the seasons. In the winter, they lived in villages of 100 to 200 people sharing twenty to thirty homes. When spring arrived, they dispersed into smaller groups and fished. Spring and early summer were the harshest time for them, despite the mild weather. Stored food was scarce or even gone. The smaller groups fished, hunted, and foraged while they waited for their crops to grow.

Powhatan bark house

During the summer they returned to their villages to care for their crops, which were mostly beans, maize (corn), and squash. They lived in oval lodges built of grass mats and bark with a dirt floor. In the center of each lodge was a huge fire. The smoke escaped through a hole at the top of the lodge. Captain John Smith described the lodges as "warm as stoves but very smoky."[10] The Powhatan kept no furniture other than raised platforms for beds. They used animal pelts for comfort and warmth. During the fall, they scattered again to hunt game and collect wild roots, berries, and nuts from the woods.

The Powhatan Indians usually had enough to get by, but they didn't have the technology to grow, gather, and store large amounts of food. They seldom had surplus food to trade with the English settlers at Fort James, but they often did. They wanted European goods, such as kettles, tools, and beads. Mostly, Powhatan wanted their modern weapons.

The women did most of the work about the village, including maintaining the crops. The men hunted, fished, went to war, and built canoes. If they had free time, they played games or did as they wished. The men never helped the women. The Powhatans thought the English weak because the men tended their own crops. Of course, in the earliest days there were no women at Fort James, which the Powhatans found even odder. The native peoples of the Chesapeake Bay area never fully adapted to the English ways of life. Few became Christians as the English had hoped.

A slaver brings a man to market. Indentured servants provided the colony's labor for the first few decades. Servants eventually worked off their debt and settled their own farms and businesses. Slaves were more economical.

Chapter

Virginia's Planters

Once John Rolfe produced a blend of tobacco that pleased the European market, Virginia was safe from bankruptcy. Farmers, both tenant and company-supported, planted tobacco. Virginia's future was safe, but it was time for the colony to mature and become more like England. For that, Virginia needed families.

In 1620, ninety women arrived and colonial life stabilized, but it was tobacco that secured Virginia's future. Unfortunately, tobacco also sealed the fate of the African American presence in the New World.

According to John Smith, Virginia's first black slaves arrived on a Dutch ship in 1619.[1] John Smith wasn't in Jamestown then, but he referred to a letter from John Rolfe to Sir Edwin Sandys in which Rolfe mentioned the "20. odd Negroes"[2] in his memoirs. In addition, Virginia's 1625 census noted "twenty-three Negroes" living in the colony.[3] A century later, 30,600 blacks were living in Virginia.[4]

Black slaves weren't the main labor force at this time. Approximately three quarters of the emigrants to Virginia between 1630 and 1660 were indentured servants.[5] An indenture was a written contract signed before an emigrant boarded a ship bound for the colonies. That contract required the emigrant to work for the person paying his or her passage for a specified number of years—usually three to seven.

Male servants outnumbered women almost three to one. Servants were young, between fifteen and twenty-four years old. Most were single. Servants couldn't marry while under contract.[6]

History often brands these servants as riffraff. The truth is that most were farmers and craftsmen. Only about one-third of indentured servants were unskilled.[7]

Life for these servants wasn't much easier than the lives of the black slaves they worked beside in the tobacco fields:

- Masters could beat disobedient servants.
- Masters could sell or lend servants.
- Contracts were part of the master's estate, which meant the master could leave a servant to someone in a will.
- Servants worked six days a week.
- Servants who ran off were obliged to work longer than the original contract. The time varied, but it was typical to double the time the servant was gone.

Most Virginians worked their own land or someone else's as a hired laborer. Indians were numerous, and originally, the Virginia Company wanted to exploit them as laborers. However, white settlers wanted the Indian lands, not their labor. Of course, the Indians resisted. In March 1622, the Powhatans massacred 347 colonists.[8] As a direct result, James I canceled the company's charter, due to mismanagement, and Virginia became a royal colony.

The Powhatans tried again in 1644. Over the next two years, the Powhatans killed at least 500 colonists. Peace finally came in 1646, when the 2,000 remaining Powhatans moved to reservations.

With peace within his sight, Governor Sir William Berkeley began work on Virginia's first plantation house in 1645. It was the first of many built by Virginia's new class—the planter class. Planters acquired new land and used slave labor to work it. Small farmers were unable to compete. By 1700, the term *planter* was interchangeable with *gentleman*.

An engraving of the 1622 massacre from a 1628 book containing conjectural images of the New World. Sixteen years after the first settlers founded Fort James, the English were an unstoppable force. New settlers claimed Powhatan hunting grounds as farm land. Warriors fought back by killing over 300 colonists, but the colony persisted.

Land was the key. The governor chose his councillors from families who owned large tobacco plantations. They, in turn, enacted laws that benefited themselves.

Virginia's planters copied England's social rules. In church, families sat according to rank. Families arranged marriages. The eldest son inherited his father's estate. Daughters received large dowries when they married.

White servants met Virginia's labor needs until the mid-1660s. After that, fewer white servants emigrated to Virginia. Land was difficult to acquire, so those who did emigrate chose Pennsylvania or the Carolinas. Virginia's planters turned to black slaves to work their fields. In 1680, about 7 percent of Virginians were black slaves. Forty years later, in 1720, 13 percent of the Chesapeake population was black.[9]

Small farmers began to push west of the established Tidewater plantations. They served as a buffer between the natives and the civilized gentry. Hostile Indians often attacked the backcountry settlers, who were plowing up their hunting grounds. Taxes were high, especially on tobacco, which was their main crop. Markets were in Tidewater, which required a long and laborious journey either downriver or through the rough terrain.

Things were about to get rough for the entire colony. English merchantmen were in financial trouble. Their ships were old and they couldn't compete with the Dutch and the Spanish. Trying to help, Charles II passed the Navigation Act of 1660. This law required all colonies to trade only with England. In addition, they had to use English ships to export all their goods to England. The act quickly destroyed competition and prices, and the price of tobacco plummeted.

Governor Berkeley, and all of Virginia, knew the act would destroy Virginia's economy. In London during 1660, Berkeley tried to convince Parliament and Charles II of the danger the act posed to Virginia:

> "if it shall appear that neither are advantaged by it, then we cannot but resent, that forty thousand people should be impoverish'd to enrich little more than forty Merchants, who being the only buyers of our *Tobacco*, give us what they please for it, and after it is here, sell it how they please; and indeed have forty thousand servants in us at cheaper rates, than any other men have slaves."[10]

He asked the king to ease the Navigation Acts a bit. He suggested an exception to the acts that would allow colonial ships to transport goods to any port they pleased. All Berkeley got for his troubles was permission to levy a two-shilling export duty on every hogshead of tobacco. From this tax, he could pay his salary of a thousand pounds a year. He was free to use the remainder to promote new products and crops for export to England. In the end, Charles II sent Berkeley back to Virginia with orders to promote hemp, flax, and silk, and to grow less tobacco.

Back in Virginia, planters were unwilling to invest in crops other than tobacco. Most alarming were the conflicts between the small farmers to the west and the native peoples. This issue, more than any other, put Berkeley at odds with Virginians.

When Berkeley refused to allow settlers in the backcountry to protect themselves from hostile Indians, the settlers rebelled. They called on Nathaniel Bacon to lead them. For most of the summer and fall of 1676, Bacon's volunteers fought Berkeley's troops and Indians. Bacon's rebels even burned Jamestown.

The immediate result was minimal. Several rebels forfeited their lives and their estates to the colony. The king recalled Berkeley in disgrace. However, this rebellion was one of the first signs that colonists weren't compliant to English rule. Some historians believe that Bacon's Rebellion planted the seeds of revolution in the American colonies.

When Nathaniel Bacon confronted Governor Berkeley, he demanded an officer's commission so that he could fight hostile natives along the colony's borders.

Colonists wanted the right to protect settlements from hostile natives. When Governor Berkeley refused to give his permission, some colonists rebelled, and even burned Jamestown.

The Virginia that followed the rebellion was no longer a tiny frontier trying to maintain some measure of society. The settlers rebuilt Jamestown, but it never recovered. In 1699, Middle Plantation (Williamsburg) became the new capital of Virginia.

Bacon's Rebellion

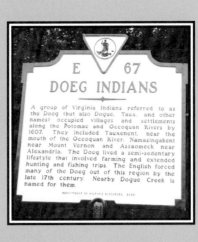

In July of 1675, a small party of Doeg Indians raided a frontier plantation and killed two men. The militia pursued the raiders into Maryland and killed a dozen Doeg Indians. They also killed a number of friendly Susquehannocks, by mistake. The Susquehannocks retaliated by attacking small settlements along the Maryland and Virginia frontiers.

Virginians went to Berkeley for help. Instead of acting decisively, he waited for the General Assembly to meet. In March of 1676, Governor William Berkeley presented a plan, which called for reinforcements along the frontier. However, troops would need the governor's permission to engage hostile Indians. Settlers rejected Berkeley's plan and asked Nathaniel Bacon, one of Berkeley's most outspoken opponents, to lead them. Bacon agreed, and in doing so, became an outlaw.

That June, the assembly passed twenty acts, which they called Bacon's Laws. Perhaps the most impressive was the act that removed tax exemptions on assembly members. For years, the ruling class had exempted themselves from most taxes.

On June 23, Bacon and five hundred volunteers surrounded the statehouse at Jamestown. Bacon demanded that Berkeley allow him to fight the hostile Indians. Calling Bacon a rebel and a traitor, Berkeley pulled his sword and challenged Bacon, who refused to fight the old man. Instead, Bacon ordered his men to fire on the statehouse. Berkeley gave in to Bacon's demands.

By early September, eight hundred of Bacon's men occupied Jamestown. When Berkeley agreed to pardon the entire bunch, he was able to retake Jamestown without firing a single shot.

Bacon was furious, but he died suddenly on October 26, 1676, before he could react. Without Bacon, the revolt was over. By January 1677, Berkeley was in full control of Jamestown. He hanged all the rebel leaders for treason. Other rebels lost their estates.

In the end, no one gained much from the rebellion. England recalled Berkeley and repealed Bacon's Laws. Berkeley died unexpectedly on July 9, 1677. Few in England or Virginia mourned him.

Governor Alexander Spotswood was a royal appointee, but he was sensitive to the colonists. He was one of the first to realize the potential of expanding the colony west into and beyond the Blue Ridge Mountains.

Chapter

(5)

From Colony to Commonwealth

After a century of colonization and cultivation, Virginia was a lot like England. That was good news to the settlers. From the very beginning, settlers and investors had intended to re-create English society in Virginia.

Plantations dotted the rivers that flowed into the Chesapeake Bay, and rich white men ran the colony. Many men inheriting plantations at this time had been born in the colony, unlike their parents. Educated in England, these sons returned to a safer Virginia than the one their parents had tamed. After Bacon's Rebellion, there was no local Indian population. By exploiting the lower classes and the colony's representative government, they increased their family wealth.

Planters did little work themselves. Slaves and servants provided labor to keep their estates running smoothly. The main goal of most planters was to acquire more land, more servants, and more slaves. Most of them accomplished that goal by purchasing land from bankrupt farmers or by marrying the daughters of nearby planters. As historian Kathleen Brown notes: "Marriage was vital to class formation and gentry identity. It was one of the primary means by which Virginia's planters maintained their dominance for the rest of the century. Through strategic intermarriages, wealthy families reaffirmed their social position and launched their sons in prominent political careers. Their daughters, meanwhile, gained economic security and a release from some of the manual labor that characterized the lives of less wealthy and enslaved women."[1]

After marriage, the wife of a planter spent her time pursuing the finer things in life: buying luxurious furnishings for her home, buying fine clothing, entertaining other planters, and supervising her servants. Unlike her husband, she spent most of her time at home or attending public gatherings such as church and private parties at other plantations. Planters' wives didn't appear in public without an escort, so they had few opportunities to socialize.

Around 1725, plantation homes became larger and grander. Brown continues, "A man's house revealed his vision of his place in the world as he wished it to be: it declared his cultural and economic ties to England, his preeminence in colonial society, and his authority over members of his household, including the slaves who generated his wealth."[2]

By dominating the area, these elite planters pushed small farmers westward into the eastern foothills of the Blue Ridge Mountains. In 1716, Governor Alexander Spotswood led a group of friends from Williamsburg to explore these mountains. Traveling from Williamsburg, they visited with settlers along the frontier. Life was much harder for these settlers than for the planters living in Tidewater. Their living conditions were similar to those of the earlier Jamestown settlers. They were far from settlements and neighbors, and they had to rely on themselves for almost everything.

From the top of the Blue Ridge, Spotswood's group gazed down the western slope. They knew that they were the first white colonists to see the green valley and the winding river the Shawnee Indians called Shanando (which means "daughter of the skies"). Spotswood named the valley and river Shenandoah. Beyond the valley, the mountains stretched as far as they could see. Spotswood's men made their way down into the valley where Spotswood claimed the land for George I.

The news of the rich Shenandoah Valley spread quickly, but it took ten more years to entice settlers to move there. Finally, Virginia offered four hundred acres to any colonist who would move into the valley. Quakers, Mennonites, and the Scotch-Irish from Pennsylvania and New Jersey moved from the northern colonies into the valley. By the time eastern Virginians arrived, they found many established homes and farms.

Once again, white settlers upset the balance of life for the native peoples. White settlers plowed up the Indians' hunting grounds for farmland. At first, the Indians resisted. They killed many settlers and burned their homes.

The French took advantage of the conflict in the valley and built a fort on the Allegheny River, in British territory. Virginia's lieutenant governor, Robert Dinwiddie, sent George Washington to confront the French. The French refused to leave.

The next year (1754), Washington returned to the fort on the Allegheny with troops. While Washington's troops battled the French at Great Meadows, Indians swept through the valley, killing the English settlers.

The French and Indian War raged on the colonial frontier for almost nine years. During that time, few English settlers were willing to venture into the valley. Westward expansion all but stopped until 1763, when the British and French signed a peace treaty. Unfortunately, at least for England, the treaty didn't put an end to the unrest in the colonies.

After the French and Indian War, England restricted colonization past the Blue Ridge Mountains. The peace treaty gave the land west of the mountains to the Indians. Then, in 1765, British Parliament passed the Stamp Act. This law called for a special stamp on all legal documents. It taxed wills, business contracts, newspapers, calendars, and even playing cards! King George III hoped the tax would pay for the cost of the French and Indian War.

American colonists complained loudly and fiercely. They even sent representatives to Parliament to protest, but Parliament ignored them.

Patrick Henry encouraged Virginians to resist the Stamp Act. Loyalists accused Henry of treason, but he didn't back down. Colonists refused to buy English goods that were taxable under the new law. Patriots organized and protested in the streets. King George did the only thing he could do. He repealed the Stamp Act in 1766.

King George and Parliament quickly enacted a new tax on tea. This time, citizens in Boston rioted. In Williamsburg, members of the House of Burgesses met to discuss the turmoil in Boston. Governor Lord Dunmore, a Loyalist, closed the assembly to try to control the rebellion in Virginia. It didn't work. The members just moved to Raleigh Tavern, where George Washington called for a boycott of English goods and slaves.

A simple boycott wasn't enough for some colonists. On December 16, 1773, angry colonists dumped tea into the Boston Harbor—342 chests of it. News of the Boston Tea Party spread quickly. On December 27, a group of 8,000 Philadelphians met a tea ship at the city's dock. The captain of the *Polly* turned his ship around and left port.

Parliament passed the Coercive Acts (called the Intolerable Acts in the colonies). British troops occupied Boston and closed the city's port. They allowed ships to unload only essential goods, such as medicine and ammunition (for the British troops). The port would remain closed until the colonists paid for the tea.

Virginia and the other colonies sent food and supplies to the beseiged city. Other royal governors closed their assemblies, as Governor Dunmore had done in Virginia.

There was no turning back for the colonists now. Virginians called for a meeting. Every colony but Georgia sent a representative to Philadelphia for the First Continental Congress. Thomas Jefferson and Patrick Henry represented Virginia. From September 5 through October 12, 1774, the colonists debated their options: More negotiations with England or war?

After colonists at Lexington, Massachusetts, challenged British soldiers on April 18, 1775, Virginia's Patrick Henry sent out a call to arms. Over fifty Virginian minutemen answered the call. They were a rough bunch. They brought their own tomahawks and knives, which they secured in their belts. The words *Liberty or Death* were sewn on their green hunting shirts and at the top of their flag. A coiled rattlesnake with twelve rattles filled the center of their flag. The warning *Don't Tread On Me* read below the snake. The snake's head represented Virginia, and the rattles were the twelve remaining colonies.

Patrick Henry stands before the Virginia House of Burgesses, giving his call to arms, "Give me liberty or give me death."

During the Second Continental Congress, Virginia's Richard Henry Lee moved "that these united colonies are, and of right other to be, free and independent states."[3] John Adams of Massachusetts seconded the motion. It was June 7, 1776.

On July 4, 1776, members of the Continental Congress approved the Declaration of Independence. Written by Virginian Thomas Jefferson, this document declared the colonies free of England's rule. The Declaration of Independence referred to the American colonies as the United States of America. Benjamin Franklin, John Adams, Roger Sherman, and Robert Livingston all worked with Jefferson to compose the Declaration of Independence. Jefferson is credited with having written the majority of the document.

Seven Virginians signed the Declaration of Independence: Richard Henry Lee, Francis Lightfoot Lee, Thomas Jefferson, Benjamin Harrison, George Wythe, Thomas Nelson, Jr., and Carter Braxton. Another famous Virginian, General George Washington, commanded the Continental Army. The fiery Patrick Henry became the first governor of the Commonwealth of Virginia.

Frontier Life

Colonial kitchen with spinning wheel

By the time Virginia became a state, most settlers living west of Tidewater still lived in log cabins. Glass was scarce, so they used shutters to secure the windows from bad weather and at night. The front door usually opened into a large kitchen with a fireplace. They ate at a wooden table with a few stools or benches. Most likely, the only other furniture was a spinning wheel. Some cabins had a second room or a small second-story loft for sleeping. Most settlers cooked, ate, and slept in the same small room.

The women prepared their food—bacon, venison, port, chicken, cornbread, and homemade jam—in huge iron pots over an open fire. They ate from wooden or pewter dishes and used wooden spoons. Afterward, they sat near the huge fireplace and talked. If they were lucky, they might sip hot coffee flavored with a bit of maple sugar and fresh cream.

Without a mill to grind their corn, they used a homemade grater. They punched holes in a tin disk. Then they nailed the disk to a block of wood, with the jagged edges of the holes pointing up. They scraped dried corn across the edges to make their cornmeal, which was a staple in their diets.

Shoes were hard to come by, and most wore moccasins made from a single piece of leather. More often than not, settlers went barefoot.

Frontier women were usually good with a rifle. Sometimes she might hunt for supper while her husband worked in the fields. Often, she helped protect her family from hostile Indians. When necessary, she worked the fields with her husband and children. A frontier woman could plow and plant, slaughter hogs and cattle, harvest crops, make and mend the family's clothes, cook meals, and keep the cabin clean. On the frontier, everyone worked, including the children, who gathered firewood and fresh water.

Chapter Notes

Chapter 1
Finding Virginia

1. David Freeman Hawke (editor), *Captain John Smith's History of Virginia* (Indianapolis, Indiana: The Bobbs-Merrill Company, Inc., 1970), p. 24.
2. Ibid.
3. Ibid., p. 25.
4. Warren M. Billings, *The Old Dominion in the Seventeenth Century: A Documentary History of Virginia, 1606–1689* (Chapel Hill: The University of North Carolina Press, 1975), p. 22.
5. Hawke, p. 24.
6. Ibid., p. 24.

Chapter 2
For Honor, Glory, and Profit!

1. Alan Taylor, *American Colonies* (New York: Penguin Books, 2001), p. 120.
2. Ibid., p. 120.
3. Wesley Frank Craven, Ph.D., *Dissolution of the Virginia Company: The Failure of a Colonial Experiment* (Gloucester, Massachusetts: Peter Smith, 1964), p. 1.
4. Ibid., p. 34.
5. Ibid., p. 33.
6. Ibid., p. 301.

Chapter 3
Virginia, "Earth's Onely Paradise"

1. Warren M. Billings (editor), *The Old Dominion in the Seventeenth Century: A Documentary History of Virginia, 1606–1689* (Chapel Hill: The University of North Carolina Press, 1975), p. 22.
2. Bernard W. Sheehan. *Savagism and Civility: Indians and Englishmen in Colonial Virginia* (Cambridge, England: Cambridge University Press, 1980), p. 11.
3. David A. Price. *Love and Hate in Jamestown* (New York: Alfred A. Knopf, 2003), p. 28.
4. Billings, pp. 25–26.

5. Ibid., p. 118.
6. Ibid.
7. Alan Taylor, *American Colonies* (New York: The Penguin Group, 2001), p. 134.
8. Richard L. Morton, *Colonial Virginia* (Chapel Hill: The University of North Carolina Press, 1960), p. 52.
9. Ibid., pp. 57–58.
10. David Freeman Hawke (editor), *Captain John Smith's History of Virginia* (Indianapolis, Indiana: The Bobbs-Merrill Company, Inc., 1970), p. 7.

Chapter 4
Virginia's Planters

1. Wesley Frank Craven, *White, Red, and Black* (Charlottesville: The University Press of Virginia, 1971), p. 77.
2. Ibid., p. 78.
3. Ibid., p. 77–78.
4. Kenneth Morgan, *Slavery and Servitude in Colonial North America: A Short History* (New York: New York University Press, 2001), p. 30.
5. Ibid., p. 8.
6. Ibid., p. 13.
7. Ibid., p. 19.
8. Ibid., p. 2–7.
9. Ibid., p. 30.
10. Warren M. Billings, *Sir William Berkeley and the Forging of Colonial Virginia* (Baton Rouge: Louisiana State University Press, 2004), p. 145.

Chapter 5
From Colony to Commonwealth

1. Kathleen M. Brown, *Good Wives, Nasty Wenches, and Anxious Patriarchs* (Chapel Hill: University of North Carolina Press, 1996), p. 249.
2. Ibid., p. 250.
3. Richard Heffner, *A Documentary History of the United States* (New York: Signet Classic, 2002), p. 6.

Chronology

1576 Martin Frobisher searches for the Northwest Passage.

1578 Sir Humphrey Gilbert founds an English colony at Newfoundland, but it doesn't last.

1585 Sir Walter Ralegh founds a small colony off the coast of modern-day North Carolina. The men abandon it quickly.

1587 Sir Walter Ralegh founds Roanoke.

1590 John White returns to Roanoke to find it abandoned.

1606 James I grants a charter to the Virginia Company of London to colonize Virginia on April 10. The Virginia Company of London's first expedition to colonize the Chesapeake Bay area left London on December 20.

1607 The expedition reaches the Chesapeake Bay on April 26. The settlers establish Fort James on a small peninsula in the James River on May 13. Late in May, hostile Indians attack the small settlement. They wound many and kill at least one settler. John Smith meets the great chief Powhatan and his daughter Pocahontas on December 30.

1608 In early January, Captain Newport returns from England with supplies to find only 38 settlers still alive. A fire destroys most of the fort on January 7. The council elects John Smith president in July.

1609 The company replaces the council with a governor. John Smith returns to England in early October. The Starving Time begins in late fall and lasts until early summer of 1610. Only 60 of 500 settlers make it through that tragic winter of famine.

1610 Jamestown settlers decide to abandon the fort, but Governor De La Warr arrives with supplies.

1612 Settler John Rolfe begins experimenting with tobacco.

1614 John Rolfe and Pocahontas marry on April 5. Seven-year term for first settlers expires.

1617 Pocahontas dies in England on March 21 at the probable age of 22.

1618 Powhatan dies in spring. The headright system is established. Virginia Company of London is 9,000 British pounds in debt.

1619 Governor Yeardley convenes the first meeting of the Virginia House of Burgesses on July 30. The first black slaves arrive.

1620 Ninety women arrive at Jamestown.

1622 Powhatan Indians massacre 347 settlers on March 22.

1624 James I revokes the company's charter on May 24.

1644 Powhatan Indians attack Virginia settlements.

1645 Governor Sir William Berkeley begins work on the state's first plantation house.

1646 Peace between Virginians and Powhatan Indians is finally reached, the Indians move to reservations.

1660 Charles II passes the Navigation Acts.

1675 Doeg Indians attack frontier plantation, eventually sparking Bacon's Rebellion.

1676 Assembly passes Bacon's Laws in June. Nathaniel Bacon dies on October 26.

1677 England recalls Governor Berkeley and repeals Bacon's Laws.

1699 The General Assembly moves the capitol to Williamsburg (Middle Plantation).

1716 Governor Alexander Spotswood leads an expedition of gentlemen to the Shenandoah Valley.

1753 George Washington warns the French at the Allegheny River to leave English territory.

1754 George Washington takes troops to confront the French at the battle of Great Meadows, beginning the French and Indian War.

1763 The French and Indian War ends with a peace treaty restricting expansion past the Blue Ridge Mountains.

Timeline in History

1492	Christopher Columbus finds the North American continent.
1506	Christopher Columbus dies.
1558	Elizabeth I is crowned Queen of England and Ireland.
1562	Jean Ribault establishes Huguenot colony at Port Royal, South Carolina (Charles Fort). They abandon the settlement in less than two years.
1565	The Spanish establish St. Augustine in Florida.
1572	Sir Francis Drake becomes a privateer.
1580	Sir Francis Drake completes his voyage around the world.
1602	Captains Bartholomew Gosnold, Bartholomew Gilbert, and Gabriel Archer explore the coast of New England.
1603	James I succeeds Elizabeth I.
1610	Henry Hudson finds the Hudson Bay.
1618	Sir Walter Ralegh is executed.
1620	The Puritans found Massachusetts, landing at Plymouth Rock.
1623	John Wheelwright founds New Hampshire.
1634	Lord Baltimore founds Maryland.
1635	Thomas Hooker founds Connecticut.
1636	Roger Williams founds Rhode Island.
1638	Peter Minuit and the New Sweden Company found Delaware.
1653	Virginians found North Carolina.
1663	Royal Charter founds South Carolina.
1664	Lord Berkeley and Sir George Carteret found New Jersey. The Duke of York founds New York.
1682	Quaker William Penn founds Pennsylvania.
1732	James Oglethorpe founds Georgia.
1764	Parliament passes the Sugar Act.
1765	Parliament passes the Stamp Act, but repeals it a year later.
1769	Daniel Boone leaves North Carolina for Kentucky.
1773	Boston Patriots organize the Boston Tea Party.
1774	Delegates meet for the First Continental Congress.
1775	Delegates meet for the Second Continental Congress.
1776	Congress adopts the Declaration of Independence.
1783	The Revolutionary War officially ends.
1789	Virginian George Washington becomes the first president of the United States. The U.S. Constitution is ratified. The French Revolution begins.
1803	The United States buys Louisiana from the French.
1812	The War of 1812 is fought against the British.
1838	The United States Army relocates 15,000 eastern Native Americans to Oklahoma. Their journey will come to be known as the Trail of Tears.
1848	Workers at Sutter's Mill in California discover gold.

Further Reading

For Young Adults

Barrett, Tracy. *Growing Up in Colonial America*. Brookfield, Connecticut: The Millbrook Press, 1995.

Butler, Amy. *Virginia Bound*. New York: Clarion Books, 2003.

Fisher, Ron. *Blue Ridge Range: The Gentle Mountains*. Washington, D.C.: National Geographic Society, 1992.

Hakim, Joy. *From Colonies to Country*. New York: Oxford University Press, 1999.

Langguth, A. J. *Patriots: The Men Who Started the American Revolution*. New York: Simon and Schuster, 1988.

Pobst, Sandra, with Kevin D. Roberts, Ph.D. *Virginia: 1607–1776*. Washington, D.C.: National Geographic Society, 2005.

Works Consulted

Billings, Warren M. *The Old Dominion in the Seventeenth Century: A Documentary History of Virginia, 1606–1689*. Chapel Hill: The University of North Carolina Press, 1975.

———. *Sir William Berkeley and the Forging of Colonial Virginia*. Baton Rouge: Louisiana State University Press, 2004.

Billings, Warren M., John E. Selby, and Thad W. Tate. *Colonial Virginia: A History*. White Plains, New York: KTO Press, 1986.

Breen, T. H. *Tobacco Culture: The Mentality of the Great Tidewater Planters on the Eve of Revolution*. Princeton, New Jersey: Princeton University Press, 1985.

Brown, Kathleen M. *Good Wives, Nasty Wenches, and Anxious Patriarchs*. Chapel Hill: University of North Carolina Press, 1996.

Carr, Lois Green, Philip D. Morgan, and Jean B. Russo (edited by). *Colonial Chesapeake Society*. Chapel Hill: The University of North Carolina Press, 1988.

Craven, Wesley Frank, Ph.D. *Dissolution of the Virginia Company: The Failure of a Colonial Experiment*. Gloucester, Massachusetts: Peter Smith, 1964.

Craven, Wesley Frank. *White, Red, and Black*. Charlottesville, Virginia: The University Press of Virginia, 1971.

Fischer, David Hackett, and James C. Kelly. *Bound Away: Virginia and the Westward Movement*. Charlottesville: University Press of Virginia, 2000.

Hawke, David Freeman (editor). *Captain John Smith's History of Virginia*. Indianapolis, Indiana: The Bobbs-Merrill Company, Inc., 1970.

Heffner, Richard. *A Documentary History of the United States*. New York, New York: Signet Classic, 2002.

Morgan, Kenneth. *Slavery and Servitude in Colonial North America: A Short History*. New York: New York University Press, 2001.

Morton, Richard L. *Colonial Virginia*. Chapel Hill: The University of North Carolina Press, 1960.

Price, David A. *Love and Hate in Jerusalem*. New York: Alfred A. Knopf, 2003.

Sheehan, Bernard W. *Savagism and Civility: Indians and Englishmen in Colonial Virginia*. Cambridge, England: Cambridge University Press, 1980.

Taylor, Alan. *American Colonies*. New York, New York: Penguin Books, 2001.

Tyler, Lyon Gardiner, LL.D. (editor). *Narratives of Early Virginia: 1606–1625*. New York: Charles Scribner's Sons, 1907.

On The Internet

Africans In America
http://www.pbs.org/wgbh/aia/home.html

Jamestown 1607: Windows to the New World
http://www.jamestown1607.org/

Jamestown Rediscovery
http://www.apva.org/jr.html

Historic Jamestowne
http://www.historicjamestowne.org/

Settler's Instructions
http://jamestown2007.org/jamestownadventure/instructions_q1.html

History of the USA: Virginia
http://www.usahistory.info/southern/Virginia.html

Politics in Colonial Virginia
http://www.history.org/Almanack/life/politics/polhdr.cfm

The Library of Virginia: Colonial Virginia
http://www.lva.lib.va.us/whoweare/exhibits/political/colonial.htm

Virginia's Historical Society
http://www.vahistorical.org/

Glossary

aristocracy
(ar-uh-STAH-kruh-see)
A class of persons holding exceptional rank and privileges, usually nobility (royal by inheritance or birth).

bankrupt
(BANK-rupt)
Having no money or means by which to pay one's debts.

cannibalism
(KAH-nuh-buh-lih-zum)
The act of a human eating the flesh of another human being.

census
(SEN-sus)
An official count of the population.

clapboard
(KLAH-bord)
Long narrow boards with one edge thicker than the other; these are overlapped horizontally to cover outer walls.

compliant
(kum-PLY-unt)
To agree and obey.

dowry
(DOW-ree)
Money and property a woman brings to her husband on their marriage.

emaciated
(ee-MAY-shee-ay-ted)
Abnormally thin; having the flesh wasted away.

gentry
(JEN-tree)
An English class just below the nobility.

hogshead
(HAWGZ-hed)
A large cask.

leadsman
(LEDZ-man)
The person responsible for measuring the depth of the water on older sailing vessels.

loyalist
(LOY-uh-list)
A person who supported the king of England and was against independence for the American colonies.

mutiny
(MYOOT-nee)
To rebel against authority, usually aboard a sailing vessel.

patriot
(PAY-tree-ut)
A colonist who wanted American independence.

persecution
(pur-suh-KYOO-shun)
An effort to kill, drive away, or enslave a people because of their race or beliefs.

pound
(POUND)
English currency, similar to the U.S. dollar.

privateer
(pry-vuh-TEER)
The captain of a merchant ship who is paid to capture supplies from enemy ships.

riffraff
(RIF-raf)
A disreputable or worthless person; a group of these people.

tenant
(TEH-nant)
A person who works land by tenure.

tenure
(TEN-yur)
A form of land ownership whereby the inhabitants retain ownership as long as they work the land. If they leave the land, they give up their rights to it.

Index